JOKES
FOR
WOMEN
ONLY

~3~

COLLECTED AND EDITED BY
SUSAN SAVANNAH

AND
SHENANDOAH PRESS

Man: What do you say to a little oral sex?

Woman: That depends. Your face or mine?

* * *

There's a new epidemic among the women in Beverly Hills. It's called MAIDS. If they don't get one, they die.

* * *

A very naive Southern girl came home after her first trip to New York and told her equally sheltered friend what she had learned there.

"Did you know," she whispered, "that up North, men kiss other men . . . down there?"

"No!" her friend gasped. "What do you call them?"

"You call them homosexuals. And they also have women who kiss other women . . . down there!"

"You're kidding!" her friend said. "What do you call them?"

"You call them lesbians. And they have men who kiss women . . . down there!"

"Well, I'll be. What in heaven's name do you call them?"

"You call them 'Darling.'"

* * *

Mom: "It's nice to see you so quiet while your Dad naps."

Little girl: "I'm just waiting for his cigarette to burn his fingers."

* * *

The football player was trying to pick up a coed at a fraternity party when she told him that she was much more turned on by academic types than by dumb party animals. "So," she said, "what's your G.P.A.?"

The jock got a big smile on his face and said, "I get about twenty-five in the city and forty on the highway!"

* * *

What does a man say after his third orgasm?

"Don't you guys believe me?"

* * *

Do you know what the worst thing about sex is?

Having to get naked in front of strangers.

* * *

My girlfriend said to me after coming home late one night, "Afterward, I feel so compromised, so cheap, so soiled . . . . so absolutely wonderful from head to toe!"

* * *

Do you know what my ex-husband uses for birth control?

His personality.

* * *

What do you call a woman with an angel for a husband?

A widow.

* * *

The Matador came home and proudly told his wife that in the arena today he was awarded the bull's ears, tail and horns.

"Next time," she says, "ask the judges for the part you could really use!"

* * *

My ex-husband was very responsible.

If anything went wrong, he was usually responsible for it.

* * *

Little girl: The teacher told us today that a single fly can lay a thousand eggs.

Mom: Yes, what about it?

Little girl: Well, I was wondering, how many can a married fly lay?

* * *

You know you've really let yourself go when they ask to check your bags and you aren't carrying any luggage.

* * *

Two women from the country were hanging out their wash when talk came around to their other neighbor, who they both considered very snooty. It seems the their neighbor's laundry never ever got rained on, so when she came out, the other two questioned her about it.

"How come," asked one, "you know when it's going to rain. Yeah," chimed in the other, "how come your wash is never hanging out on those days."

The snooty neighbor leaned over the fence and said, "It's simple. When I wake up in the morning I look over at my husband, Joey. If his penis is hanging over his left leg, I know it's going to be good weather and I come right out with my laundry. Now, if it's hanging right, it's going to rain for sure, so I hang it up inside."

"Well," the other neighbor sneered. "What's the forecast if Joey's got a hard-on?"

"Girls," the snooty neighbor said with a smile, "on a day like that you don't do the laundry."

* * *

I was told my ex gave up drinking.

He must have seen the handwriting on the floor.

* * *

Talk about impotent.

My ex couldn't even get his hopes up!

* * *

"Man, that was like a religious experience!" said the young man. "Was it that way for you, too?"

"Well, almost," sighed the girl. "I was hoping for a second coming."

* * *

What's the high point of a bulimic's birthday party?

It's when the cake jumps out of the girl.

* * *

After making love, the woman said to the man, "So you're a doctor?"

"That's right," said the doctor smugly. "Do you know what kind?"

"I'd say an anesthesiologist."

"How did you know?" asked the M.D.

"Because throughout the entire procedure, I didn't feel a thing."

* * *

I was telling my friend the other day, "If my husband really loved me, he would have married someone else."

* * *

Marriage is a good way for a woman to keep active until the right man comes along.

* * *

I got in trouble with my husband for kissing the best man after the ceremony!

Of course, it was three years after the ceremony.

* * *

A shoe salesman was trying to score with a woman at the front desk in the hotel where he was staying. He offered her $100 for just one hour in his room. She told him that she didn't do it for money, only for love.

This didn't faze the super salesman. He told her that he had some beautiful designer shoe samples that she really ought to see. She reluctantly agreed and when she got to his room and saw the shoes, she fell in love with a stunning pair of red pumps.

"Well," she said, "I don't get turned on by this kind of thing, but you can give it your best shot."

They got undressed and the salesman started pumping away, confident that she would succumb to his sexual skills. He tried everything, but she was just lying there. After awhile he felt one arm wrap around him and then a leg. He redoubled his efforts, and soon he felt the other arm and leg around him.

"You thought I wouldn't get to you, eh?" he smirked. "Admit it. I'm the best fuck you've ever had, right?"

"Don't kid yourself," she said calmly. "I'm just trying on my new shoes."

* * *

You notice there are no sex changes from women to men.

That would be a demotion.

* * *

What would they call an operation like that?

An ADD-A-DICK-TO-ME.

* * *

I'm satisfied with my boyfriend. As a matter of fact, I've had all I want of him!

* * *

I always hate myself afterwards . . .

But before and during — WOW!!!!

* * *

I met my husband at a party.

I almost shit. I thought he was home with the kids.

* * *

"Adultery," shouted the hand-waving evangelist, "is as bad as murder! Now, isn't that so, Sister Brown?"

"Don't rightly know, parson," answered Sister Brown. "I ain't never killed nobody."

* * *

It's one of the great mysteries of life.

How men can get older but still manage to remain so immature.

* * *

A man whose wife had tired of him sexually finally talked her into going to a hypnotist for treatment. After a few visits to the 'Doctor,' she returned home and everything was exactly as it was when the couple were on their honeymoon.

He was puzzled, however, by the fact at different times during their lovemaking his wife would dash out of the bedroom. After she got up the third time, he tip-toed after her to the bathroom. There she was standing before the mirror, staring at herself and repeating over and over, "It's not my husband . . . . it's not my husband."

* * *

Three girlfriends were out bar hopping one night when after quite a few drinks, one suggested they tell one another something they'd never told anyone else. "All right," said one of the girls, "you first."

"OK," she said as she took a deep breath, "I've never told anyone I'm gay."

When she recovered from the shock, the second woman confessed, "I'm having an affair with my husband's best friend."

"Well," the third one began, "I don't know how to say this . . . . ."

"Go on," the two others said, "Don't be embarrassed."

"Well," she said, "I can't keep a secret."

* * *

How many husbands does it take to change a light bulb?

One — to hold the bulb and wait for the world to revolve around him.

* * *

For women, marriage has its ups and downs.

The toilet seat is up, and your sex life is down.

* * *

Women don't make passes

at men who are asses.

* * *

How do you keep a man from wanting sex?

Marry him.

* * *

Marriage is like a violin.

After the music is over, you still have the strings.

* * *

An attractive middle-aged woman, dressed in the team colors and obviously a big fan, was sitting in a two-seat box all alone. The usher approached her and asked, "Why is this seat empty, ma'am?"

The woman said, "It's my husband's seat."

"Where is he?"

"He died."

"Oh, well, couldn't you have given the seat to a friend or somebody in the family?"

The woman shook her head. "They're all at his funeral."

* * *

Do you know why the "900" phone sex lines are so popular?

Because when it comes to sex, most men are all talk.

* * *

He stopped calling her "the little woman" when she started to call him "the big mistake."

* * *

My last boyfriend was really cultured.

He would go down on me, and tell me I smelled like caviar!

* * *

What has 75 balls and screws little old ladies?

Bingo.

* * *

Three co-workers discovered that they all had new boyfriends with the same name. They decided, to avoid confusion, to nickname them after soft drinks.

"I'll name mine Seven-up," said the first one. "He's about seven inches and always up."

The second one said, "I'll name mine Mountain Dew, because he loves my mountains and he sure can do it."

"I'll name mine Jack Daniel's," said the third.

"You can't do that," said her friends. "That's not a soft drink, that's a hard liquor."

"He sure is!" she said.

* * *

There are two days when a man is a joy; the day one marries him, and the day one buries him.

* * *

At the marriage counselor's office, the woman complained, "What's-his-name here says I don't give him enough attention."

* * *

Divorce is the future tense of marriage.

* * *

"Your husband looks a little on the heavy side."

"He's heavy on every side!"

* * *

My ex-husband was a pig at the dinner table.

I used to tell him, "When you get to the white part, that's the tablecloth."

* * *

My ex got on the rowing machine one night and it sank!

* * *

There was a horrible mistake at the hospital, and a man who was scheduled for a circumcision was given a sex-change operation. The doctors gathered at his bed afterwards and told him the bad news.

The patient started sobbing. "Jesus," he wailed, "I'll never be able to experience an erection again."

"Of course you'll be able to experience an erection again," said one of the surgeons, "but it will have to be someone else's."

* * *

My ex-husband's new girlfriend had to quit wearing hoop earrings.

She kept getting her high heels stuck in them.

* * *

My girlfriend complains that her lover is too fast in bed.

She says she never gets a piece's minute from him!

* * *

You're the world's worst lover!" the husband growled.

"I couldn't be," his wife shot back. "That would be just too much of a coincidence!"

* * *

One of my silly-assed neighbors told me the other day, "Whenever I'm down in the dumps I buy myself a dress."

I've always wondered where she got them!

* * *

What's the difference between a husband and a boyfriend?

About 60 pounds!

* * *

In the latter stages of my marriage, food became more important than sex to my husband.

In fact, he had the walls of the dining room lined with mirrors!

* * *

I fixed up a girlfriend with a gentleman friend of mine who happens to be very old. When I asked her how it went, she said, "I had to slap his face three times!"

"Did he get fresh?" I asked.

"No, I thought he was dead!"

* * *

I asked my girlfriend what sign her boyfriend was.

She said, "Taurus with penis rising."

* * *

When you get older, you can appreciate the finer things in life.

You can't do any of them, but you can appreciate them!

* * *

The two were in a motel room getting undressed when the girl said, "You sure don't say much."

"Nope." said the guy as he pulled down his shorts. Pointing, he says, "I do all my talking with this."

"Jesus!" she said. "Is that all you have to say?"

* * *

My ex-husband wasn't a very good communicator.

It's hard to drink beer and talk at the same time.

* * *

A woman tells her co-worker, "I can't break my husband of the habit of staying up till five in the morning."

"What is he doing?" her friend asks.

"Waiting for me to get home."

* * *

Excited Husband: Quick, honey, I just got my semi-annual hard-on.

Incredulous Wife: You mean you just got your annual semi-hard-on.

* * *

While touring some factories in the U.S., a British businessman was forced by bad weather to stay over in a rundown hotel in the bad part of town. He thought he could write some letters to pass the time. He went to the front desk and asked the girl who was working, "Do you keep stationary?"

"Yeah," she answered, "until someone touches my clit. Then I go fuckin' crazy."

* * *

What's the difference between your ex-husband and a football?

You only get three points for kicking a football between the uprights.

* * *

Here's a new ad campaign for batteries:

Lover never ready?

Rely on Eveready!

* * *

Do you know why women have a higher threshold of pain?

So they can put up with men.

* * *

We all know that diamonds are a girl's best friend.

We also know that man's best friend is a dog.

Now you tell me. Which is the smarter sex?

* * *

My ex-husband is a born again cretin!

* * *

My ex is uncircumcised.

The doctors were afraid of brain damage.

* * *

Did you ever hear a guy say, "I'd do her in a minute!"

We need to tell them that this is part of the problem.

* * *

My marriage is childless, except for my husband.

* * *

Did you know that any woman can have the body of a 21-year-old.

You just have to buy him a few drinks first.

* * *

Sometime in the future, a Alien couple swap spouses with an Earth couple. When they were alone, the Alien male undressed, and the woman from Earth noticed that his organ was quite small. He then wiggled a finger in his ear and his penis lengthened rapidly. When he did the same thing to his other ear, it began to thicken.

When they were all finished, the Earth woman asked her man how it was.

"It wasn't all that good," he said. "Not only did the Alien woman have a huge vagina, but she distracted me while we were doing it by tickling my ears like crazy!"

* * *

What do gay men and straight men have in common?

They both hate women.

* * *

When we started out, my ex and I decided we wanted to keep growing as people.

I just never imagined he would grow to 300 pounds!

* * *

My husband and my appendix operation had some amazing similarities.

They both caused a lot of pain, and once they were removed, I found out I didn't need them anyway!

* * *

What do men and beer bottles have in common?

They're both empty from the neck up.

* * *

The widow was talking to the funeral director the day after her husband's death. "What would you like to say in the obiturary?" he asked her.

"Goldstein died," she said.

"That seems a little short. You really should have at least five words."

"All right," she replied. "How about 'Goldstein died. Cadillac for sale'?"

* * *

My ex-husband tried to become a sex fiend, but he couldn't pass the physical!

* * *

I knew my ex-husband was cheating on me.

I knew where and I knew with whom.

What I never could figure out was . . . . . with what?

* * *

I think I made a Freudian slip the other morning.

I was having breakfast with my husband, and what I meant to say was "Sweetheart, will you please pass the milk." But what came out instead was, "You asshole, you've really fucked up my life."

* * *

I had to take my boyfriend to the doctor the other day.

He had an ingrown beer can.

* * *

One housewife asked another about her husband working with asbestos every day. "You know," she said, "it could cause impotence. Aren't you afraid he'll lose the lead in his pencil?"

"Big deal," the woman said. "He doesn't do all of my writing, anyway."

* * *

What's the difference between being married and childbirth?

One is an excruciatingly painful, almost unbearable experience.

And the other is just having a baby.

* * *

My ex used to make the worst hamburgers in the world.

I could never eat mine, so I used them to clean the sink!

* * *

Money can't buy happiness.

It just helps you look for it in more places.

* * *

When I get serious about a certain guy, I think to myself, is this the man I want my children to spend their weekends with?

* * *

I had to kill my analyst.

He helped me alot, but he knew too much.

* * *

A young woman was complaining to her friend about her boyfriend's amazing sex drive. "I hardly have the strength to go to work in the morning," she said. "Now that he's off on holiday, things will only get worse."

"How long is he off?" her friend asked.

"Usually," she said, "just time enough for one cigarette."

* * *

My girlfriend who was a stewardess, says her husband is mad at her because the other night when he nudged her awake, she murmured, "Welcome aboard."

* * *

My mother, who is sixty-five, confided in me that she was having an affair.

"Really?" I said, "Who's the caterer?"

* * *

How many men does it take to screw in a light bulb?

One. Men will screw anything.

* * *

If women knew how men pass the time when they are alone, they'd never marry!

* * *

What's the difference between a poodle humping your leg and a pit bull humping your leg?

You let the pit bull finish.

* * *

What's the difference between savings bonds and men?

Savings bonds mature.

* * *

Why do men always give their penis a name?

Because they don't want a stranger making 95 percent of their decisions for them.

* * *

I saw my friend the other day and she had her wedding ring on the wrong finger. When I pointed this out to her she said, "I know, I married the wrong man."

* * *

Life still offers fun and excitement when your old . . .

It just offers them to younger people.

* * *

When the man first noticed that his penis was growing longer, he was delighted. But several weeks and several inches later, he became concerned and went to see a urologist.

While his wife waited outside, the physician examined him and explained that, though rare, his condition could be corrected by minor surgery.

The patient's wife anxiously rushed up to the doctor after the examination and was told of the diagnosis and the need for surgery.

"How long will he be on crutches?" she asked.

"Crutches?" the doctor asked.

"Well, yes," the woman said. "You are going to lengthen his legs, aren't you?"

* * *

The man sadly told his wife the bad news. He had cancer and had only a few months to live.

"You could make my final days happier," he said, "by giving me something you have always denied me — oral sex."

His wife agreed and began satisfying him.

A month later, the man went for a check-up.

After examining him, the doctor asked if he had been taking any new drugs or doing anything unusual.

"Well," he said, "my wife has been giving me daily blow jobs."

"That must be it," the doctor said. "You're completely cured!"

When the elated man told his wife, she began to cry. "What is it, dear?" he asked.

"I can't help thinking," she sobbed, "I could have saved John Wayne."

* * *

My boyfriend and I have what we call Smurf Sex.

That means screwing until you're blue in the face!

* * *

Do you know why psychoanalysis takes longer for women than men?

When it's time to go back to childhood, men are already there.

* * *

My ex-husband should have his ears cleaned out.

With a gun!

* * *

Two married women meet on the street. One says, "What am I going to do? My husband doesn't know how to drink. He doesn't know how to play poker. What am I going to do?"

The other woman said, "I don't know why you're complaining."

The first woman says, "Because he drinks and he plays poker!"

* * *

Why do men resist becoming fathers?

Because they aren't through being children.

* * *

My friend and I have a gay dentist.

We call him the tooth fairy!

* * *

While the man was undressing in the motel room, the girl lit up a cigarette.

"You shouldn't smoke," he said, "those things will stunt your growth."

"Don't you ever smoke?" she asked.

"Never," he replied as he was taking off his shorts.

"So," she said, lowering her gaze, "what's your excuse?"

* * *

Meanwhile, back at the oasis, the Arabs were eating their dates.

* * *

How can you tell if your husband is happy?

Who cares?

* * *

If you want to find out what life is like without a man around . . . just get married.

* * *

I have a new way to do it doggie-style.

I put on my sexiest teddy and then make my boyfriend roll over and beg.

* * *

I didn't know my ex-husband drank until he came home sober one night!

* * *

JOKES
FOR
WOMEN
ONLY'S

NAUGHTY & BAWDY
LIMERICKS
(OH NO!)

There was a young man named Ringer,
Was seducing a beautiful singer.
  He said with a grin,
  "Now, I've got it in."
She said, "You mean that isn't your finger?"

* * *

There was a young lady of Wheeling
Who professed to a lack of sexual feeling.
  But a cynic named Boris
  Just touched her clitoris,
And she had to be scraped off the ceiling.

* * *

There was a young man from St. Paul
Whose cock was exceedingly small.
    Now it might do for a keyhole
    Or a little girl's peehole.
But for a big girl like me — not at all.

* * *

There was a young girl from Cheshire
Who succumbed to her lover's desire
    She said, "It's a sin,
    But now that it's in,
Could you shove it a few inches higher?"

* * *

There was a young lady of Dexter
Whose husband exceedingly vexed her,
    For whenever they'd start
    He'd unfailingly fart
With a blast that damn nearly unsexed her.

* * *

A gentle old lady I knew
Was dozing one day in her pew;
    When the preacher yelled "Sin!"
    She said, "Count me in!
— And as soon as the service is through!"

* * *

There was a young man from Australia
Who painted his ass like a dahlia.
    The colors were fine;
    The drawing — divine!
But the smell was a terrible failure!

* * *

There was a young lady from Kent —
When her husband's pecker it bent,
    She said with a sigh,
    "Oh, why must it die?
Let's fill it with Portland Cement."

* * *

A pansy by name of Ben Bloom
Took a lesbian up to his room
    They talked the whole night
    As to who had the right
To do what, with which, and to whom.

* * *

There was a young woman of Croft
Who played with herself in a loft,
    Having reasoned that candles
    Could never cause scandals,
Besides which they never went soft.

* * *

There was a young fellow named Fyfe
Whose marriage was ruined for life,
  For he had an aversion
  To every perversion
And only liked screwing his wife.
Well, one year the poor woman struck
And she wept, and she cursed at her luck,
  "Oh, where has it gotten us
  This goddamn monotonous
Fuck after fuck after fuck?"

* * *

"It is time," said a woman from Devon,
"To exchange maiden bliss for sex heaven.
    There is music, it's spring,
    Flowers bloom, birdies sing;
And besides, I've just turned thirty-seven."

* * *

There was a young sailor named Bates
Who danced the fandango on skates.
    But a fall on his cutlass
    Has rendered him nutless,
And practically useless on dates.

* * *

There was an old maiden named Grissing
Who discovered what she had been missing.
    When laid down on the sod,
    She cried out, "Oh, God!
All these years I just used it for pissing!"

* * *

~ FINAL THOUGHT ~

I was taught to believe that all men are created equal.

Then I went to an orgy.

* * *

Do you know any good

'JOKES FOR WOMEN ONLY?'

If so, send them to:

Shenandoah Press

8070 La Jolla Shores Dr.

#460

La Jolla, CA 92037-3230

Remember, there can be no compensation,
but your favorite jokes and stories will be
immortalized in print!

Thanks again,

S.S.

ORDER
BY
MAIL

CLIP OUT COUPON.

Indicate which and how many
books you want to order.

Enclose a check or
money order payable to:

Shenandoah Press
for $6.50 per book.
(Price includes postage,
sales tax and handling.)

MAIL TO

Shenandoah Press
8070 La Jolla Shores Dr., #406
La Jolla, CA 92037-3230

NAME _____

ADDRESS _____

CITY _____ STATE _____ ZIP _____

PLEASE SEND ME:

☐ JOKES FOR MEN ONLY

☐ JOKES FOR WOMEN ONLY

☐ MORE JOKES FOR WOMEN ONLY

☐ JOKES FOR WOMEN ONLY 3

JOKES FOR WOMEN ONLY ~3~ SAVANNAH

COUPON

NAME _____

ADDRESS _____

CITY _____ STATE _____ ZIP _____

PLEASE SEND ME:

☐ JOKES FOR MEN ONLY

☐ JOKES FOR WOMEN ONLY

☐ MORE JOKES FOR WOMEN ONLY

☐ JOKES FOR WOMEN ONLY 3

JOKES FOR WOMEN ONLY ~3~ SAVANNAH